3 0132 01954122 1

D0188164

Northumberland Schools Library Service	
3 0132 01954122 1	
Askews	Oct-2010
S741 RED	£11.99

21st CENTURY LIVES
CARTOON CHARACTERS

Paul Mason

WAYLAND

First published in 2010 by Wayland

Copyright © Wayland 2010

Wayland
338 Euston Road
London NW1 3BH

Wayland Australia
Level 17/207 Kent Street
Sydney, NSW 2000

All rights reserved.

Editor: Julia Adams
Designer: Rebecca Painter
Picture researcher: Shelley Noronha

Picture Acknowledgments:
p1: (rpt p18) Entertainment Pictures/Photoshot; p4: Everett Collection/Rex Features; P5: David
James/Warner Bros/Courtesy of Warner Bros./Bureau L.A. Collection/Corbis; P6 & COVER:
Entertainment Pictures/Photoshot; p7: ComedyC/Everett Collection/Rex Features; p8: Entertainment
Pictures/Photoshot; p9:Entertainment Pictures/Photoshot; P10 & COVER: Entertainment
Pictures/Photoshot; p11: Entertainment Pictures/Photoshot; P12 & COVER: Entertainment
Pictures/Photoshot; p13: 20thC.Fox/Everett Collection/Rex Features; p14: Entertainment
Pictures/Photoshot; p15: Entertainment Pictures/Photoshot; p16: Entertainment Pictures/Photoshot;
p17: Marvel/Sony Pictures/The Kobal Collection; p18: Entertainment Pictures/Photoshot;
p19 Warner Bros/DC Comics/The Kobal Collection/James,David; p20: Everett Collection/Rex
Features; P21: Jordan Strauss/WireImage/Getty Images

Mason, Paul.
  Cartoon characters. -- (21st century lives)
  1. Cartoon characters--Juvenile literature.
  I. Title II. Series
  741.5-dc22

ISBN: 978 0 7502 6202 6

Printed in China

Wayland is a division of Hachette Children's Books, an Hachette UK·company

www.hachette.co.uk

Contents

Batman
Bat-inspired Crime Fighter

Batman swings into action in Batman: The Animated Series, which ran from 1992–95.

"By the spirits of my parents, [I will] avenge their deaths by spending the rest of my life warring on all criminals."

A young Bruce Wayne makes the promise that will ultimately turn him into Batman, standing beside the graves of his parents. They had been killed days before.

Name: Batman/Bruce Wayne

Nicknames: The Caped Crusader, The Dark Knight, The Bat.

Description: By day, a wealthy industrialist and partygoer; by night, a vigilante crime fighter.

First appeared: May 1939, in issue 27 of Detective Comics.

Creator: Bob Kane (writer) and Bill Finger (artist)

Friends: Superhero sidekick Robin, butler Alfred, and Police Commissioner Gordon

Foes: The Joker, The Penguin, Two-Face, The Riddler, and Catwoman (among others)

Background: Batman is a famous superhero – without any superpowers! Instead, he relies on his intelligence and physical training to defeat criminals.

Career milestones: Batman began life as a comic-book character in 1939, but has also appeared in TV shows (from 1966); a cartoon series called *Batman: The Animated Series* that started in 1992; and a series of movies: Tim Burton's *Batman* in 1989, then *Batman Returns* (1992), *Batman Forever (1995)*, *Batman and Robin* (1997), *Batman Begins* (2005) and *The Dark Knight* (2008).

You might not know: Bruce Wayne's name is a combination of two others: famous Scottish king Robert the Bruce, and American War of Independence hero General Anthony Wayne.

Batman surrounded by some of his bat-brothers (and sisters) in *Batman Begins*, released in 2005.

Batman first appeared as a cartoon character in May 1939. His character was written by Bob Kane, and the drawings were done by Bill Finger. Batman's story begins with a murder. On the way home from a Gotham City movie theatre, young Bruce Wayne's parents are shot dead by a robber. Standing beside their grave, the eight-year-old boy vows to free Gotham of the epidemic of crime that has led to his mother's and father's death.

Bruce returns to his family home, Wayne Manor, and begins training himself. At first, he does not know how he should hide his true identity when he goes crime fighting:

"My disguise must be able to strike terror into [criminal] hearts. I must be a creature of the night, black, terrible…" At just that moment, a bat flies past his window. "A bat! That's an omen. I shall become a bat!" Batman has been born.

Bruce Wayne/Batman becomes an expert at fighting, and develops various devices that will help him fight crime. Many of these will eventually appear on his famous Bat-belt, which Batman always wears. They include weapons such as Batarangs, throwing weapons like boomerangs; Bat-grenades, which are used to stun enemies; and Bat-darts, with knockout drops on the tips. The Bat-belt is also equipped with Bat-cuffs for locking up criminals, and a Bat-hook, which hooks on to tall buildings, so that Batman can climb them.

The one thing missing from Batman's belt is a gun. He refuses to carry a weapon like the one that killed his parents. Batman has a whole range of vehicles to help him fight crime: a Batboat, a Batsub, a Batcycle, and – most famous of all – the Batmobile.

When Batman is needed, the police send up a signal – the Bat-signal – asking him to come and help. Bruce heads for the Bat-cave, deep underground below Wayne Manor, and emerges as Batman – ready to do battle with whatever criminals await.

Today, Batman is one of the most successful cartoon characters ever. The TV shows, Hollywood movies, Batman toys and games – and of course the cartoons themselves – have made him famous around the world.

"People fantasize about being a hero and helping someone in trouble. Batman is that fantasy… not just for Bruce Wayne, but for the audience".

Kevin Conroy, the voice of the cartoon Batman, explains why he thinks the character has been popular for such a long time.

Eric Cartman
Unpleasant Fourth-grader

Eric Cartman – usually known as "Cartman" – plots another evil deed.

"I'm not fat! I'm big boned!"

Cartman's often-repeated explanation of why he's heavier than everybody else his age.

Name: Eric Theodore Cartman

Nicknames: Often called The fat one, or The fat kid.

Description: A deeply unpopular student at South Park Elementary School, Colorado (USA), who nonetheless manages to convince himself that he is the most popular kid in school.

First appeared: 1995 (in 'The Spirit of Christmas'); first South Park episode 13 August 1997.

Creators: Trey Parker and Matt Stone

Voiced by: Trey Parker

Friends: Cartman doesn't really have friends, but he hangs out with Stan, Kyle, and Kenny

Foes: Wendy Testaburger, Scott Tenorman, all hippies, everything to do with *Family Guy*

Background: Cartman is famous for his unpleasant schemes to humiliate his enemies, and his crackpot plans for making money.

Career milestones: A Cartman-like character first appeared in a 1992 short cartoon called *The Spirit of Christmas*, although in it he was named Kenny. The Cartman of today first appeared in 1995, in a second *Spirit of Christmas* cartoon. He has been a member of the cast of *South Park* since the show began on 13 August 1997.

Cartman is also a singer and action hero. He sings on the music albums *Chef Aid: The South Park Album*, and *Mr Hanky's Christmas Classics*, and appears in four *South Park*-related video games.

You might not know: Cartman is partly based on an old friend of Trey Parker and Matt Stone (the creators of *South Park*), named Matt Karpman. Amazingly, the three are still friends.

Cartman misbehaves in the *South Park* episode "Die, Hippy, Die". "Hippies" are one of the things Cartman most dislikes.

The Eric Cartman the world knows and loves first hit our screens on 13 August 1997. He is the creation of animators Trey Parker and Matt Stone. Eric Cartman is an unpleasant, rude, selfish, spoiled fat kid with no real friends. Despite this, he has managed to become one of the most popular cartoon characters of all time.

Fans of the show in which Cartman stars, *South Park*, have thrilled at his triumphs, such as when he managed to get himself temporarily made a policeman. Cartman spent his time as a cop patrolling South Park on his Big Wheel tricycle, using a police baton to attack the shins of people who refused to obey him.

Cartman's fans have also witnessed his lows, such as his terrible experience of thinking he was dead: all the other kids started ignoring him after he ate every single skin off a bucket of fried chicken, before anyone else had had any. Cartman also has to put up with constantly having his demands that people, "Respect my authority!" ignored. Through it all, though, his fans stand by their favourite fourth-grader.

Cartman lives at home with his mum, Liane Cartman. Cartman orders his mum around. If he doesn't get what he wants immediately, he starts either shouting or whining at her. In the end, Cartman usually gets his way. Cartman is equally badly behaved at school, where he hangs around with Stan, Kyle, and Kenny. Many of Cartman's schemes are aimed at Kyle, who he dislikes. He also dislikes Stan's girlfriend, Wendy Testaburger.

Despite being someone you wouldn't actually want to know in real life, Cartman regularly features in lists of the best-ever cartoon characters. His movies, TV shows, albums, and countless T-shirts, bags, mugs, models and other merchandise have made Cartman a worldwide celebrity.

Karate instructor: "Cartman-san! What are you doing?"
Cartman: "I'm doing some sweet banzai moves. I'm a little better than everyone else here."

Karate instructor: "Eric-san, you must follow direction! You lack discipline!"

Philip J Fry
Saviour of the World

Philip J Fry

> **"I'm never gonna get used to the 31st century. Caffeinated bacon? Baconated grapefruit?"**

Fry complains about life – and particularly breakfast – a thousand years from now.

Name: Philip J Fry

Nicknames: Usually known as just Fry.

Description: A pizza delivery boy from 1999 who is cryogenically frozen, so that 1000 years later he will be able to save the world.

First appeared: 28 March 1999

Creator: Matt Groening

Voiced by: Billy West

Friends: Turanga Leela, Professor Hubert J Farnsworth, Bender

Foes: The Brainspawn, the Dark Ones

Background: Fry is a nice-but-dim character who, when he travels back and forth through time, accidentally becomes his own grandfather. This results in him lacking the 'Delta brainwave' – which in the year 2999 counts as a superpower, sort of.

Career milestones: Fry appeared in the first episode of *Futurama*, in March 1999. The series has kept appearing on our TV screens, sometimes with big gaps, ever since: the most recent programmes were released in 2010.

Of course, as a big star, Fry doesn't only appear in one TV show. There have been four *Futurama* feature films. Fry also stars in *Futurama Comics*, a comic book set in the world of *Futurama*, and in various games, including video games.

You might not know: Before he became a pizza delivery boy, Fry had spent the previous three years indoors watching TV.

Fry gets a girlfriend! Unfortunately, she's a virtual human he has downloaded from the Internet, and the romance doesn't last long.

Soon after being brought back to life, Fry meets careers adviser Turanga Leela. He once again finds work as a delivery boy – this time, though, Fry's deliveries take him around the universe, not just around New New York City. He's working for Planet Express, an intergalactic delivery company. Planet Express is owned by Fry's only living relative – his 160-year-old nephew, Professor Hubert J Farnsworth.

Fry's work-mates at Planet Express include Leela, who has given up her job as a careers officer; her pet, Nibbler; Bender, a bad-tempered robot who cannot help himself stealing other people's possessions; and Professor Farnsworth, who started Planet Express to provide money for his crazy science experiments.

The Planet Express team has many adventures together, but their greatest come when Fry saves the Earth – which he does twice. First, Fry's lack of the 'Delta brainwave' makes him immune to attacks from the evil Brainspawn, who plan to destroy the universe. In *The Why of Fry*, he blows up the Brainspawn base, the Infosphere, using a Quantum Interface Bomb. Then, when a group of mysterious, evil beings called the Dark Ones plan to destroy all life in the Universe in the movie *Into The Wild Green Yonder*, only Fry is able to stop them. Fry, Leela and the rest of the team are last seen heading for a 'wormhole' that Professor Farnsworth warns could transport them trillions of light years away. As the Planet Express slides into the hole, Fry's fate is uncertain.

Fry stars not only in *Futurama*, the TV show, but also in a series of comics and movies. He also appears on all kinds of merchandise, from T-shirts to baseball caps.

Philip K. Fry was created by Matt Groening for the cartoon series *Futurama*. Fry first hit the world's screens in March 1999. He is a New York City pizza-delivery boy with a difference. On New Year's Eve 1999, he is out on a delivery when he accidentally falls into a cryogenic pod. The pod freezes him for a thousand years, before finally setting him free on New Year's Eve, 2999.

The New York (now called New New York) that greets Fry is very different from the one he last saw: humans, aliens and robots live side by side (the alcohol-powered robots are now the biggest cause of global warming); wheels no longer exist – people get around using hover cars or a network of clear, air-powered transportation tubes. Earth has a single government. Its president is the head of former US President Richard Nixon, which has been preserved in a jar since his death. Although it lacks a body, Nixon's head – like many others that have also been preserved – can think and talk.

"Fry, it is my solemn duty to inform you that the fate of humanity, the fate of our race, indeed, the fate of all that exists and ever will exist, rests with you. You are the most important person in the universe."

Philip J Fry learns his true purpose in the 31st century.

Turanga Leela
Spaceship Captain of the Future

Turanga Leela: the roughest, toughest former careers officer in the thirty-first century.

"After all this time, somebody else with one eye... who isn't a clumsy carpenter or a kid with a BB gun."

Leela finally meets another Cyclops (person with one eye in the middle of their forehead). He turns out to be a fake.

Name: Turanga Leela

Nicknames: Usually known as just Leela, but sometimes Clobberella.

Description: Leela is the hard-fighting martial-arts expert who captains the Planet Express spaceship in *Futurama*.

First appeared: 28 March 1999

Creator: Matt Groening

Voiced by: Katey Sagal

Friends: Philip J Fry, Nibbler, Bender

Foes: Captain Zapp Branigan (sometimes), the Brainspawn, the Dark Ones

Background: Leela's intelligence and ability mean that she is the one who most often gets the crew of the Planet Express out of trouble. Although tough, she has a softer side: Leela loves both weapons and animals.

Career milestones: Leela appeared in the first episode of *Futurama*, in March 1999. The series has been popular ever since, with the latest episodes released in 2010.

You might not know: Leela gets her name from a piece of classical music called the Turangalîla Symphony, by Olivier Messiaen.

Turanga Leela stunned cartoon fans when she first appeared in March 1999. How could someone with one big eye in the middle of her forehead be such a babe? Blame creator Matt Groening. Leela's story begins in an 'orphanarium', the thirtieth-century version of an orphanage. She has been abandoned there as a baby, along with a note in an alien language saying, "Your parents love you very much." With her one eye and otherwise-perfect humanoid features, people can see immediately that she is one of the many aliens that now live on Earth.

Fast-forward the story to the year 2999, and Leela has a job as a Career Placement Officer for Recent Defrostees at a cryogenics facility in New New York City. She assigns jobs to people who have recently been brought back to life. This is how Leela meets Philip J Fry, to whom she gives the job of delivery boy.

Leela takes a terrified-looking Fry for a whiz around the New York City of the thirty-first century.

Fry refuses his new job – he has already been a pizza delivery boy in his previous life. He flees into the city, with Leela in hot pursuit. They team up with a robot called Bender, and find Fry's only living relative, Professor Farnsworth. Leela and Bender hate their current jobs, so all three sign up as the crew of the Professor's delivery spaceship, Planet Express.

Leela is quickly made captain – Bender is violent and unpredictable, and Fry is not intelligent enough. Almost straight away Fry falls for Leela, but she keeps turning him down for dates. Instead she goes out with a series of unsuitable characters, including Alcazar, who she thinks is another Cyclops but who turns out to be a shapeshifting impostor.

Leela later discovers that she is not, in fact, an alien orphan. Instead she is the child of two one-eyed sewer mutants, who was born "the least mutated mutant ever." Earth's sewer mutants live only in the sewers

and never come to the surface. Leela's parents decided to leave her outside the orphanarium to give her the chance of a normal life.

Whether Leela's life is 'normal' or not is uncertain – but either way, she remains one of *Futurama's* biggest stars. As one of *Futurama's* best-loved characters, Leela appears on everything from fan websites to plastic lunchboxes. She is also, of course, a big star in the five *Futurama* movies that made up the show's fifth season.

"[Leela is a] tough, strong career girl who just can't get it together in the rest of her life… she's vulnerable and hard at the same time."

Katey Sagal, the voice of Leela in *Futurama*.

Bart Simpson
Mischievous Elementary Student

As you would expect from a big star, Bart relaxes in his director's chair. (He takes the sunglasses off when he's acting.)

❝I don't know! I don't know why I did it, I don't know why I enjoyed it, and I don't know why I'll do it again!❞

Bart Simpson

Name: Bartholomew JoJo Simpson

Nicknames: Bart

Description: Bart is the naughty but loveable oldest son of Homer and Marge Simpson. His trademark phrases include: "Eat my shorts", "Ay caramba!" and "Don't have a cow, man."

First appeared: 19 April 1987 on *The Tracey Ullman Show*, 17 December 1989 on *The Simpsons*.

Creator: Matt Groening

Voiced by: Nancy Cartwright

Friends: Millhouse Van Houten

Foes: Moe at Moe's Tavern, Principal Skinner, Ms Krabappel and Groundskeeper Willlie

Background: Bart is a ten-year-old student at Springfield Elementary School. His rebellious personality and refusal to obey orders make him unpopular with adults – but very popular with his fans.

Career outline: Bart and the rest of the Simpson family first appeared in a cartoon that was part of another TV show, *The Tracey Ullman Show*. After three years they moved on to their own programme, *The Simpsons*, which quickly became one of the most popular and successful cartoons ever.

You might not know: Every Simpsons character is named after someone from the family of the show's creator, Matt Groening – except Bart. Bart's name is made of the letters from the word 'brat'.

Appearing in *The Simpsons Movie*, an under-dressed Bart leaps over outraged citizens on his skateboard.

When he first drew Bart Simpson, Matt Groening couldn't have imagined he was creating one of the most successful cartoon characters of all time. Bart first appeared in April 1987, it was not long before he and his family rocketed to world fame.

"I am dumb, OK?" Bart says one day. "Dumb as a post! Think I'm happy about it?" Bart certainly doesn't do very well at school, where he is constantly in trouble either with his teacher Ms Krabappel, or Principal Skinner. In one episode of *The Simpsons*, Bart's sister Lisa even manages to prove that he's more stupid than a hamster. But even if he is stupid, Bart has plenty of great achievements to his name. These include getting his best friend Milhouse Van Houten placed on the FBI's Most Wanted Criminals list. But Bart's greatest triumph was probably reuniting his favourite TV star, Krusty the Clown with Krusty's long-lost father, and getting Krusty's show put back on the air after it had been ended by the TV channel.

Sadly, Bart's relationship with his own father, Homer, is not great. Bart regularly drives Homer into a crazy rage, often deliberately, and ends up being picked up and strangled as a result. Unfortunately, both Homer and Bart have the 'Simpson gene' – a part of their physical makeup that means all men in the Simpson family are stupid. Fortunately, Bart's mother Marge is cleverer and kinder than her husband, and Bart knows he can usually turn to her for help.

One of Bart's favourite tricks is to phone Moe, the bartender at Moe's tavern, and ask to speak to someone with a made-up name:
"Hello," Bart says, "Is Oliver Clothesoff there?"
"Hang on, I'll see," Moe replies, before asking if Oliver Clothesoff is in the room. When Moe realizes he's been tricked by a comedy name, he goes mad with rage.

As well as starring in *The Simpsons*, Bart became the subject of 'Bartmania'. He appears on millions of T-shirts, mugs, posters, stickers and other products. He also raps on the song 'Do The Bartman', which was written for him by Michael Jackson.

Bart's cartoon career has turned him into a major showbiz player: *Time* magazine included him in its list of the 100 Most Important People of the Twentieth Century, and in 1990 he was named Entertainer of the Year by *Entertainment Weekly*. Bart and the rest of his family have made *The Simpsons* one of the most successful, longest-running shows in TV history.

"My standard comment is, if you don't want your kids to be like Bart Simpson, don't act like Homer Simpson."

The Simpsons creator Matt Groening responds to claims that Bart sets a bad example to kids.

Lisa Simpson
Super-brainy Sister

Lisa Simpson

> " Bart, having never received any words of encouragement myself, I'm not sure how they're supposed to sound. But here goes: I believe in you. "
>
> **Lisa Simpson**

Name: Lisa Marie Simpson

Nicknames: no nicknames

Description: Lisa is the cleverest member of the Simpson family. Although they fight, she and her brother Bart are also very close.

First appeared: 19 April 1987 on *The Tracey Ullman Show*, 17 December 1989 on *The Simpsons*.

Creator: Matt Groening

Voiced by: Yeardley Smith

Inspirations: Her grandmother, Mona Simpson, and jazz musician 'Bleeding Gums' Murphy.

Dislikes: Animal cruelty and sex discrimination

Background: Lisa is the eight-year-old second child of Homer and Marge Simpson. She is a vegetarian, a feminist and a Buddhist, and supports human rights and environmental campaigns.

Career outline: When she first appeared on TV, Lisa was a bit like a younger, female version of her naughty brother, Bart. However, it soon became clear that Lisa was a lot cleverer than Bart: we now know that she has an IQ of 156. Lisa is a bit of a misfit: her vegetarianism and environmentalism make her very unusual in her family.

You might not know: Lisa has won several Genesis Awards for her animal-rights campaigning.

Lisa in *The Simpsons* episode 'She of Little Faith', doing Buddhist chanting with... yes, that is Richard Gere!

Lisa is also different from the rest of her family (and most of the town of Springfield) because of her beliefs. She is a vegetarian (someone who does not eat meat) and an animal-rights supporter. One day Lisa even throws a can of red paint over Krusty the Clown, Bart's favourite entertainer, because he is wearing a fur coat. Lisa is a Buddhist, and follows the Noble Eightfold Path to Enlightenment. None of the other Simpsons understand exactly what this is – especially her dad, Homer, and Bart.

Even though they are so different, and sometimes fight, Bart and Lisa are good friends. They enjoy making prank calls to Moe's together:
Bart (with Lisa): "Is Mister
Freely there?"
Moe: "Who?"
Bart: "Freely, first initials I. P."
Moe: "Hold on, I'll check. Uh, is
I. P. Freely here? Hey everybody,
I.P. Freely!"

When she's not making calls to Moe's with Bart, or hanging out with her super-clever Mensa friends, Lisa is often found practising her saxophone. She loves music, especially the jazz musician 'Bleeding Gums' Murphy. Murphy teaches Lisa to express her emotions through music, and when he dies, he leaves her his saxophone.

When Matt Groening first came up with the character of Lisa Simpson, she was like a smaller, female version of her older brother Bart. But not long after her first appearance in April 1987, it started to become clear that Lisa was a most unusual member of the Simpson family – a super-brainy one.

Unlike her brother Bart, Lisa loves school and is good at her lessons. In fact, during a teachers' strike when she is unable to go the Springfield Elementary, Lisa gets "school withdrawal". She becomes so desperate that she ends up begging her mum to give her a grade for something. Lisa gets her brains from her grandmother on Marge's side, Mona Simpson. She is so clever that she becomes a member of the Springfield branch of Mensa (a society for specially intelligent people).

As one of the show's main characters, Lisa plays a major role in *The Simpsons Movie*. She also sang "Moanin' Lisa Blues" and "God Bess The Child" on the *The Simpsons Sing The Blues* album, and has appeared on The Simpsons Ride at Universal Studios, Orlando, Florida.

"Lisa Simpson can't wait for college. She's only 8 and already reads at a 14th grade level… If she could have one thing (besides world peace), it would be a pony."

Description of Lisa Simpson at www.thesimpsons.com

Spiderman
The First Teenaged Superhero

Spiderman, battling crime high above the city streets.

> **Who am I? You sure you want to know? The story of my life is not for the faint of heart. If somebody said it was a happy little tale... if somebody told you I was just your average ordinary guy, not a care in the world... somebody lied.**

Spiderman introduces the story of his life.

Name: Spiderman/Peter Parker

Nicknames: Spidey

Description: In normal life, a student and freelance photographer for the *Daily Bugle*; as a superhero, a mysterious rescuer of those in distress and preventer of crimes.

First appeared: August 1962, in issue 15 of *Amazing Fantasy*.

Creator: Stan Lee (writer) and Steve Ditko, (artist)

Friends: Aunt May and Uncle Ben, and his friend and sweetheart Mary Jane Watson

Foes: Green Goblin (the killer of Peter Parker's first real girlfriend, Gwen Stacey), Doctor Octopus, Hobgoblin, Mysterio, and Electro

Background: Spiderman is a teenaged superhero, who struggles to accept that his special powers mean he will never be like the people he protects.

Career outline: Spiderman, like all the original superheroes, started life as a comic-book character. He has since also appeared in several cartoon series, TV shows, books and computer games. Today he is most famous for three films starring Tobey Maguire and Kirsten Dunst, released between 2002 and 2007.

You might not know: *Spiderman: Turn Off The Dark* is a musical based on the story of Spiderman and Peter Parker. The songs are written by Bono and The Edge from the rock band U2.

Spiderman has a dark twin! This scene is from the 2007 movie *Spiderman III.*

magnified many times. Not only can Spiderman climb across ceilings: he also has many other powers. They include climbing sheer walls, leaping vast distances, and firing threads from his wrists that allow him to swing like Tarzan from building to building. He also has a "spider sense", which alerts him to danger, and super-human strength, speed and agility.

Peter keeps his powers secret, even from Uncle Ben and Aunt May, who brought him up after his parents were killed in a car accident. He makes a spider costume that keeps his true identity secret, and at first uses his new skills to become a massive TV star. Then one day at the studio, Peter refuses to use his spider-powers to capture a thief, saying it's the police's job, not his. The thief later kills Uncle Ben, and – as Spiderman – Peter vows that from now on he will fight crime wherever he finds it.

When he goes to college, Peter shares a room with Harry Osborne, and the two become friends. But Harry's father turns out to be Spiderman's greatest enemy, the Green Goblin. The Goblin attacks Spiderman in whatever ways he can.

Peter Parker regularly finds it difficult to juggle the demands of being a superhero with trying to live a normal life. This is especially so when people he loves are attacked and hurt by his enemies. At one stage he even decides to give up being a superhero, but fortunately for the people of New York City, he changes his mind.

Through his long career, Spiderman has appeared in comic books, cartoons, TV shows, computer games and, of course, movies. If that's not enough for Spidey fans, they can also play Spiderman computer games, eat from Spiderman lunchboxes and go to sleep wearing Spiderman pyjamas – under a duvet cover featuring their favourite superhero.

Before Stan Lee first imagined the character of Spiderman, superheroes were all grown-up men. Lee imagined (and Steve Ditko drew) the first teenaged superhero, who appeared in August 1962.

Peter Parker is an unlikely superhero. In fact, you couldn't imagine anyone less like a superhero! He's a weedy (if brilliant) science geek, who is constantly picked on by the school bullies. In particular, Flash Thompson takes great delight in calling him "Puny Parker," and never misses a chance to humiliate him.

Then, one day during a science demonstration, Peter's life changes forever when he is bitten by a radioactive spider. At the time, Peter thinks little of it, but the next morning, he wakes up upside down, clinging to the ceiling of his bedroom. He soon realizes that he has somehow taken on the radioactive spider's powers,

"With great power comes great responsibility."

Spiderman/Peter Parker's Uncle Ben explains why Spiderman has to use his powers to help people.

Superman
Alien Superhero

Superman in the 1996 TV show
Superman: Last Son of Krypton

"I'm here to fight for truth, and justice, and the American way."

Superman

Name: Superman/Clark Kent

Nicknames: Man of Steel, Man of Tomorrow, Last Son of Krypton.

Description: In everyday life, a mild-mannered newspaper reporter; when danger threatens, a super-powered superhero.

First appeared: The character was invented in 1932, and first appeared in the June 1938 issue 1 of *Action Comics*.

Creator: Jerry Seigel (writer) and Joe Schuster (artist)

Friends: Lois Lane, Jimmy Olsen and Perry White of the *Daily Planet*, Superboy, Supergirl, and Krypto the Superdog

Foes: Lex Luthor of LexCorp, the Kryptonian criminal General Zod, the alien android Brainiac, and a monster called Doomsday (among many others)

Background: Superman rocketed to Earth from his home planet, Krypton, and uses his alien powers to battle for good.

Career outline: Superman began life as a character in a comic strip. He was so popular that he soon starred in a radio show, TV cartoon series, a 1950s TV show called *Adventures of Superman*, several movies, and a more recent TV show called *Smallville*.

You might not know: Superman has a motocross trick named after him. The rider does a big jump, then gets off the saddle and flies along holding on to the handlebars, with arms outstretched and legs trailing behind.

A still from the most recent Superman movie: *Superman Returns*, released in 2006.

It soon becomes clear that Clark Kent is no ordinary child: he begins to develop some amazing powers. When he is older, these include the ability to fly and to run so fast that it is impossible to see him. Clark also develops super strength; invincibility to almost any attack; amazing powers of vision (including X-ray vision, heat-ray vision, telescopic vision, and the ability to see in the dark); super-sensitive hearing and breath that can blow as powerfully as a gale, or freeze whatever it touches. Clark's parents decide that his powers must be kept secret, and should only be used for good.

As a young man, Clark goes to work for the *Daily Planet* newspaper, in the city of Metropolis. Hardly anyone knows that Clark Kent, the shy, quiet newspaperman, is actually Superman. In particular, the beautiful Lois Lane is fascinated by Superman, but not so interested in Clark. Superman soon comes across plenty of opportunities to use his powers to help people and fight crime.

The thing Superman fears most is kryptonite. This is the radioactive remains of his home planet, Krypton. Kryptonite cancels out Superman's powers, and causes such pain that he cannot move. Fortunately, there are just a few pieces of Kryptonite on Earth – so Superman can rarely be stopped from helping those who need his aid.

Today, Superman is as popular as ever, through TV shows such as *Smallville*, which tells the story of his teenage years. As a result of his fame, the Superman 'S' sign inside a triangular shield has become one of the most recognisable symbols in the world. Athletes from runners to basketball stars have it tattooed on their arms, and it appears on mugs, bags, sweatshirts and even underwear. There are Superman fans from San Francisco to Shanghai, and pretty much everywhere in between.

When Jerry Seigel and Joe Schuster first came up with the character of Superman in 1932, they never imagined how long his popularity would last. Even after Superman first appeared in print in 1938, it would have been impossible to foresee how many copycat superheroes would follow in his path.

Superman first comes to Earth as a baby, in a rocket fired from the planet Krypton moments before it is destroyed in an explosion. He is discovered by Jonathan and Martha Kent, farmers in the US state of Kansas. With no children of their own, they decide to raise the baby themselves. The Kents give him the name Clark. They bring Clark up to have a strong sense of what is right and wrong.

"Superman: faster than a speeding bullet, more powerful than a locomotive, and able to leap tall buildings in a single bound."

Description of Superman first used in the 1940s radio show in which he starred.

Ben Tennyson
Omnitrix-toting Crusader

Ben Tennyson, in the centre, flanked by his cousin Gwen and Kevin Levin.

"I've kicked so much alien butt, my feet hurt!"

Ben Tennyson in 'Hunted'

Name: Benjamin Kirby Tennyson

Nicknames: Ben

Description: An ordinary boy, Ben is able to transform himself into a range of alien life forms, using an alien-technology device he discovers.

First appeared: On 27 December 2005 in *Ben 10*; then again on 18th April 2008 in *Ben 10: Alien Force*.

Creators: Joe Casey, Joe Kelly, Duncan Rouleau, and Steven T Seagle

Voiced by: Tara Strong/Yuri Lowenthal

Friends: Gwen Tennyson, Grandpa Max, Julie Yamamoto, the Plumbers

Foes: Charmcaster, Dr Animo, Forever King, Vilgax, the Highbreed

Background: Ben uses his powers to help people, and to fight evil-doers, both from Earth and from space.

Career summary: Ben's first appearances on TV were in the show *Ben 10*, when he was 10 years old. He also starred in *Ben 10: Alien Force*, followed by *Ben 10: Evolution*.

Ben and his amazing powers have also been the stars of three feature films: *Secrets of the Omnitrix*; *Ben 10: Race Against Time*; and *Ben 10: Alien Swarm*. Finally, he is the hero of several computer games.

You might not know: Ben and his cousin Gwen are exactly the same age; they even share the same birthday.

BEN 10

RACE AGAINST TIME

A poster advertises Ben's 2007 appearance in *Ben 10: Race Against Time*.

CN CARTOON NETWORK

He picks it up and puts it on – only to discover that it's not a watch at all. It's an Omnitrix.

Ben soon discovers that the Omnitrix allows him to turn himself into 10 different alien life forms, each with its own special powers. Among them are Heatblast, who can fire streams of flame and fireballs, as well as being able to blast himself off the ground like a rocket. Ben can also become Wildmutt, an eyeless alien that 'sees' by his amazing senses of smell and hearing and is a cross between a lion, a wolf and a gorilla. XLR8 is a velociraptor-like alien with wheels as feet, that can reach speeds of 480 kilometres per hour in the blink of an eye. Fourarms is a 3.6-metre-tall, four-armed alien with armoured skin and amazing strength.

Like Spiderman (see pages 16-17), Ben finds that with great power comes great responsibility. Together with Gwen (who has mysterious powers of her own) and his grandfather, Max, Ben has many adventures fighting off attacks by human and alien enemies – in particular, the villain Vilgax.

Kids around the world daydream of being a teenage superhero like Ben. There are certainly plenty who would like an Omnitrix that can get them into and out of trouble. As a result, the Ben 10 movies are very popular, and so are the video games, clothing, and other Ben-10-branded merchandise that's available.

Ben 10 first appeared on people's TV screens at the age of 10, in 2005. After appearing in several cartoon series he disappeared – only to reappear in 2008, aged 15 (proving that cartoon time isn't like ordinary time). He was created by the Man of Action studio, and first appeared on the Cartoon Network.

Ben Tennyson's career as a superhero starts on a camping trip with his cousin Gwen and their grandfather. Ben goes off in a huff after fighting with Gwen, and stumbles across what seems to be a watch.

"You hold the key to a power struggle so ancient, so vast, it is beyond your feeble comprehension. Picture an entire army, each in command of an Omnitrix at my command: I will be invincible. I will rule the universe. And the only thing standing between me and my destiny is you."

Arch-villain Vilgax confronts Ben in 'Secrets'.

Other Cartoon Characters

Homer and Marge Simpson

Homer and Marge are the dad and mum at the head of the Simpson family, who live in Springfield, Illinois. Homer is regularly voted one of the 10 best cartoon characters of all time – despite being unintelligent, lazy, not very good at his job and overweight. Even with all his flaws, Homer is devoted to his family.

Marge Simpson has plenty to put up with: not only a husband like Homer, but also a son like Bart, her 10-year-old eldest child. She tries to keep order and make the family behave well, but it's a good job that Marge is extremely patient, as she never succeeds for long.

Stan Smith

Stan Smith stars in *American Dad!* as a Deputy-Deputy Director of America's Central Intelligence Agency (CIA). *American Dad!* was first shown on 6 February 2005. Stan's family is made up of his wife Francine, their daughter Hayley and their son Steve. He also lives with two very strange characters. The first is an alien called Roger, who once saved Stan's life. The second is a goldfish called Klaus – whose fish body contains the mind of a former East German Olympic ski jumper.

Stan is a former secret agent, trained to kill and an expert shot. He and Francine met when he picked her up hitchhiking: he ran over a squirrel and shot it to put it out of its misery. Francine thought it was the kindest thing she'd ever seen. Although he is a loving husband and father, Stan's high standards and extreme patriotism can make him hard to deal with.

Tom and Jerry

Tom (a pet cat) and Jerry (a mouse) often feature in lists of people's top three cartoon characters ever. They've been big cartoon stars since they first appeared in 1940. Jerry is always trying to get cheese, which has often been left for him as a trap by Tom. Meanwhile, Tom spends almost all his time trying to catch Jerry – but he never quite succeeds.

In the course of their chases, both Tom and Jerry get hit in the face with frying pans, have giant anvils dropped on them, get blown up in explosions and are flattened by steamrollers, among other things. Somehow they always manage to survive.

Ren and Stimpy

Ren Hoek is a crazy Chihuahua; his sort-of friend Stimpson 'Stimpy' J. Cat is a dim-witted manx cat (manx cats have no tail). The pair wander around together having strange, hard-to-understand adventures. They have been big stars since they first appeared on TV, on 11 August 1991.

Ren regularly turns into a crazy chihuahua and commits terrible violence against Stimpy. This led some parents to complain that *The Ren And Stimpy Show* wasn't suitable for the children it was aimed at.

Scooby Doo

Scooby Doo has had one of the longest careers of any modern cartoon character. Not only has he starred in his own cartoon show since 1969, but he has also appeared in at least 21 cartoon movies, and three filmed movies featuring live actors. He's even starred in several computer games.

Scooby and his friends Shaggy, Fred, Daphne and Velma travel around in their old 'Mystery Machine' bus, which is the mobile headquarters of Mystery Inc. The mysteries they investigate seem at first to involve ghosts or monsters.

In the end, though, the ghosts or monsters turn out just to be ordinary crooks. Scooby is rarely brave, but he always helps solve the case.

Bugs Bunny

Bugs Bunny, with his trademark catchphrase "What's up, Doc?", is one of the most popular cartoon characters ever. Bugs, who is actually a hare, not a bunny rabbit, first appeared alongside the useless hunter Elmer Fudd, in the cartoon *A Wild Hare*, on 27 July 1940.

Ever since, Bugs has been tormenting his rivals and enemies. These include Fudd, the Tasmanian Devil, Wile E. Coyote and Yosemite Sam. At first he tries to avoid conflict, but soon things reach a point where Bugs declares: "Of course… You know this means WAR!" Bugs takes decisive action, and his attacks are so terrible that his enemies never win.

SpongeBob SquarePants

SpongeBob SquarePants and his friends first hit the screens in May 1999. SpongeBob is a sea sponge: along with his friends Patrick Star (a starfish) and Sandy Cheeks (a squirrel), and their neighbour Squidward Tentacles (a squid), they've been a big hit with the kids ever since they first appeared.

The goings-on in Bikini Bottom, the underwater city off the coast of Florida where SpongeBob lives, have made him into a huge star. Today, he has appeared in a movie, on two amusement park rides, and on countless mugs, lunch boxes, boxer shorts, cereal packets and other products.

Fred Flintstone

Fred Flintstone is one of the main characters in the cartoon show *The Flintstones*, which first appeared in September 1960. Fred lives with his wife Wilma and daughter Pebbles, at 345 Cave Stone Road. They share their home with Dino the pet dinosaur and Baby Puss, a sabre-tooted tiger. At first Fred works as a bronto-crane operator at the local quarry, but later he and

his friend and neighbour Barney join the local police force.

Cartoons featuring Fred and the rest of the Flintstone family are still regularly shown on TV, and they have also appeared in the feature films *The Flintstones* (1994) and *The Flintstones in Viva Rock Vegas* (2000).

Mickey Mouse

Mickey Mouse was first seen on screen in *Plane Crazy*, in 1928. Not many people know it, but Mickey was very nearly called Mortimer instead. The wife of his creator, Walt Disney, convinced Walt to change the name to Mickey Mouse at the last minute.

Mickey is one of Disney's most popular and long-lived characters. He is still popular around the world today and remains the leader of *The All-New Mickey Mouse Club*. This long-running TV show has featured 'Mouseketeer' presenters including Christina Aguilera, Britney Spears and Justin Timberlake.

Wonder Woman

Wonder Woman first appeared in *All Star Comics* in December 1941. She had super-speed, super-agility and amazing powers of endurance. Her tools included a pair of bracelets that could defend against any attack, an invisible airplane and a Lasso of Truth. Anyone caught in the Lasso was completely unable to lie.

Since she first appeared, Wonder Woman has appeared in comic strips, cartoons, TV shows, books, video games and a cartoon movie. Since 2001 there have been rumours that a Wonder Woman feature film is on its way.

Index

21st Century Lives

Contents of books in the series: